Britain Since 1930

John Corn

ACKNOWLEDGEMENTS

The author and publisher would like to thank the following for permission to reproduce photographs and other material:

Allsport/Adrian Murrell	35a
British Petroleum	43a
British Rail Photographic Unit, York	38a
Camera Press	29c
Chorley and Handford Limited/Paul Proctor	37a
Environmental Picture Library	44b (Graham Burns), 45b (H. Giradet)
Hulton Deutsch Collection	4a, 4b, 5, 7a, 8/9, 10, 11b, 14a, 14b, 16, 16/17, 21, 29d, 34b, 44a
IBM United Kingdom Limited	46
Imagine/Irene Lynch	24/25
Imperial War Museum	6, 12a
International Stock Exchange Photo Library, London	18b, 19, 47a, 47c
John Corn	26b, 43b
Mansell Collection	28a
Museum of London	15
National Motor Museum, Beaulieu	40a, 40/41, 41a, 41b
NRM/Science and Society Picture Library	36
Peter Newark's Historical Pictures	7b, 8a, 9a, 11a, 17
Peter Ryan	39
Popperfoto	13, 28b
Redferns	30a, 30b, 30c, 31a (David Redfern), 31b (Ian Dickson), 31c (Susan Moore)
Retna Pictures Limited	29a
Rex Features Limited	28c, 29b, 33a, 38b
Robert Opie Collection	24a, 34a,
Royal Mint, Llantrisant	18a
Science Museum/Science and Society Picture Library	1, 32a, 32b, 47b
Syndication International Limited	25a, 25b, 35b
Tank Musuem Collection, Bovington	12b
Thomas Cook Travel Archive	37c
Thomson Tour Operations Limited	37b
Tidy Britain Group	45a
Topham	20, 22, 23, 26a, 42

© 1994 Folens Limited, on behalf of the author.

United Kingdom: Folens Publishers, Apex Business Centre, Boscombe Road, Dunstable, LU5 4RL.
Email: folens@folens.com

Ireland: Folens Publishers, Greenhills Road, Tallaght, Dublin 24.
Email: info@folens.ie

Poland: JUKA, ul. Renesansowa 38, Warsaw 01-905.

Editor: Ian Jenkins
Cover design: Design for Marketing, Ware

First published 1994 by Folens Limited.

British Library Cataloguing in Publication Data. A catalogue record for this publication is available from the British Library.

ISBN 1 85276 184-9

CONTENTS

1. The Depression

An industrial town in Britain in 1930. Towns like this were badly hit by the depression.

In the 1930s there was an economic depression all over the world. Other countries could not afford to buy British goods, so factories in Britain had to close and many people were unemployed. In some areas of Britain there were many factories close together. These areas were very badly hit by the depression.

A town called Jarrow in the north of England was one of these places. In the early 1930s an unemployed man would receive about £1.50 a week to feed his family. This was only just enough. There was no money left for anything else.

Year	Number of people out of work
1930	3,643
1931	6,603
1932	6,793
1933	7,178
1934	6,462
1935	6,053
1936	4,065
1937	3,784
1938	3,143
1939	2,342

This chart shows how unemployment increased in Jarrow in the early 1930s.

A family in 1930.

The town of Jarrow was badly hit by unemployment. In 1934, eight out of every ten men were unemployed.

Thousands of men volunteered to march to London, nearly 300 miles away, to show the people of Britain how much they wanted work. They also wanted to give a petition to the government, asking for help. Two hundred men were chosen to march.

 One of the marchers was John Harney. He wrote this poem:

We started off from Jarrow Town, a pale-faced, hungry band,
With all the population out, to shake us by the hand.
But as we left our homes behind, determination grew,
On every face, to show the world, what Jarrow lads could do.

People were very kind to the men as they marched. They were given food and shelter. In Wakefield they slept in a church, in Leicester their boots were mended free of charge. More than £680 was given to them during their march – a great deal of money in those days.

Poverty and hardship

1. Give one reason why people were out of work in Britain in the 1930s.
2. How much money did an unemployed family get from the government every week? Was it enough?
3. What happened to unemployment in Jarrow in the 1930s?
4. Write a list of words to describe the photograph of the industrial town on page 4.
5. Why did the men march from Jarrow to London? Give two reasons.
6. How far did they march?
7. £1.50 a week was hardly enough to feed a family. Look at the photograph of the family on page 4. What else do you think this family needs?

Hard times

Find out more about the depression in Britain.

1. Draw a map to show the route of the march.
2. Pretend you are John Harney. Write about the march.
3. What else could the unemployed have done?

Key ideas

depression   unemployment

The Jarrow March.

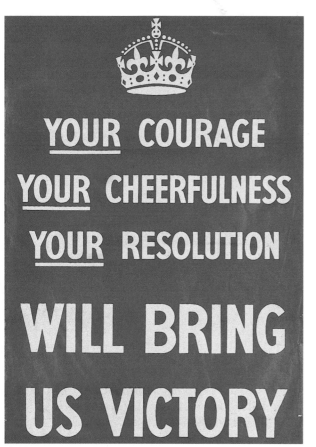

Posters like this were designed to help people in Britain stay cheerful during the war.

The war affected life in Britain in many different ways. At the beginning of the war, very little happened because Britain was not ready to fight Germany. People began to think it was a 'Phoney War'.

However, Britain slowly began to make itself ready for war. Factories and industries stopped making their usual goods and started making equipment for the army, navy and air force. Men were conscripted (made to join the armed forces). By the end of 1939, people began to see the effect of the war on their everyday lives.

The Prime Minister, Winston Churchill, and his government believed that it was important for the people of Britain to stay cheerful. Radio programmes, posters and leaflets all encouraged people to be positive and help the war effort.

2. Britain at War

On 3rd September 1939, Britain declared war on Germany. There were many reasons for this. The main reason was that Germany had invaded Poland. The people of Britain were afraid that Germany would invade and take over other countries in Europe, including Britain.

The Second World War lasted for six years, until August 1945, and involved every continent.

Everyday life

1. Why did Britain declare war on Germany in 1939? Give two reasons.
2. Make a list of the equipment that the armed forces might have needed.
3. How do you think a radio programme or a poster could make people more cheerful?
4. Look at the posters on these pages. Who are the posters aimed at?
5. What are the posters trying to say?
6. What has happened to the signposts in the photograph on page 7? Why?

Key ideas

Phoney War   Second World War
propaganda   spy

Signposts were taken down during the war in case of a German invasion.

'Spy fever' grew quickly in the early months of the war. It was forbidden to give a stranger directions. Roadblocks and observation posts were built throughout the countryside. All signposts were taken away so that if German soldiers invaded Britain, it would be difficult for them to find their way around.

Posters like this were put up during the war to stop people giving away British secrets.

Propaganda was a powerful weapon in the early days of the war. While the British government encouraged people to stay cheerful, the Germans wanted to do the opposite. They broadcast radio messages which tried to worry and frighten people in Britain by telling of German victories in the war. The messages claimed to know where German bombs were going to fall and what damage they would cause. Both Britain and Germany dropped leaflets from planes telling people to give up.

As well as propaganda, the Germans began to use spies to find out British secrets about the war. The British government wanted people to be careful when they were talking to one another in case they gave away secrets by mistake.

Propaganda

Pretend you live in Britain at the beginning of the Second World War.

1. What kinds of secrets could 'Careless Talk' give away?
2. Describe the kind of propaganda you have heard or seen (both British and German).

3. The War at Home

The people of Britain began to feel the effects of the Second World War in 1940. The 'Phoney War' had ended.

Germany wanted to take over Britain. To make the British people weak, the Germans tried to cut off supplies of food and other goods. German submarines attacked many of the ships that brought food to Britain.

The British people could produce some food themselves, but food that came from other countries was soon in short supply. To make sure that everyone had a fair share the government introduced rationing. This meant that people could have only a certain amount of food each week. Everyone was given coupons in a ration book. When people paid for their food, they exchanged coupons for the food they were allowed.

 Food was difficult to get, as Mrs Wilson from Hull remembers:

Some people used to throw a lot of food away. There was a tip not far away and when people saw the lorry they used to go and see what they could get. I remember we had quite a few tins. There was a lot of grapefruit juice but we used to get tins of spam, which were quite alright, just dented.

This painting shows a British ship being attacked by a German U-boat in 1940.

The government encouraged everyone to 'Dig for Victory' and grow their own food. Lawns and parks were dug up and planted with fruit and vegetables.

Saucepans were collected and the metal was used to build machines and equipment.

Everyone in Britain was encouraged not to waste anything and to recycle whatever they could, including food, clothing and household goods. Many women joined the Land Army and did the farming while the men were away fighting. The government thought that this 'army' was just as important as the army that was fighting Germany.

This painting from 1941 shows the amount of food that was rationed to two adults for a week.

The war effort

1. Why did the Germans attack British ships during the war?
2. What was rationing? How did it work? How important was it?
3. What do you think 'Dig for Victory' means?
4. How could growing and eating your own food help win the war?
5. What was the Land Army? How did it help the British people during the war?
6. How could collecting saucepans help Britain during the war?

Rationing

Find out how people changed their lives to help Britain during the war.

1. Look at the painting of rationed food. Find out what each type of food is and how much was given to two adults for a week.
2. What kind of meals did people eat using rationed food? How were these different to meals eaten before the war?
3. Write a shopping list for someone in 1940 under three headings: 'rationed', 'home-grown' and 'impossible to get'.
4. When did rationing end?
5. What do you think would have happened if there had been no rationing during the war?
6. Write a list of the things that people used every day during the war which could be recycled and used again in a different way.

Key ideas

Phoney War   Second World War
rationing

4. Women and Wartime

Before the Second World War, some women worked outside the home. However, many people thought their jobs were less important than men's jobs. Women worked mainly in low-paid jobs such as cleaning and factory work. Most married women did not work. They were expected to look after the house and children.

The Second World War caused great changes in the lives of all women. When men left home to join the army, navy and air force, the women who were left behind took over their jobs. They worked on farms and in factories making munitions and supplies. They drove lorries, ambulances and buses. By 1940 more than two million women were working.

 This song was written about women workers during the war:

It's the girl that makes the thing that
    drills the hole that holds the spring
That works the thingumebob that
    makes the engines roar.
And it's the girl that makes the thing that
    holds the oil that oils the thing
That works the thingumebob THAT'S
GOING TO WIN THE WAR!

A woman working in a munitions factory during the war

 Women at war

1. Write a list of the jobs done by women during the war.
2. Look at the photograph of the woman in the factory. What job is she doing? What special clothes is she wearing?
3. Who is the song about? Why do you think the song was written?
4. Why did the government make unmarried women go out to work?
5. Why are the women on page 11 marching?
6. What happened to working women after the war? Why?

 Key ideas

equal pay   munitions

Many married women wanted to work during the war, but they could not because they had to look after their children. To help these women, the government opened more nursery schools. In 1940 there were only 14 nurseries in the country. By 1944 there were 1,450.

However, there were still not enough nursery places for young children. Most mothers who wanted to work had to ask relatives or neighbours to look after their children.

In 1946, within a year of the end of the war, over a million women had left their jobs. Women at work still did not receive equal pay or equal treatment as men, but they could never be told again that there were 'men's' jobs that women were not capable of doing.

Posters like this encouraged women to work.

Many women volunteered for war work, but there were still not enough volunteers. The government decided to make unmarried women go to work. By 1943, all unmarried women aged from 19 to 51 had to work.

Working women

Find out more about women at work.

1. What was the most important job done by women during the war?
2. What jobs did women do after the war?

In 1942, mothers in London protested at the lack of nursery schools.
The lack of nurseries prevented them from doing important war work.

A government poster asking men to join the Home Guard.

5. Men and Wartime

During the Second World War most men between the ages of 18 and 45 were 'called up' for military service. They joined the army, the navy or the air force. The only men who stayed at home were those aged over 45, those who were unfit or disabled, or those with jobs that were too important to leave. These jobs were called reserved occupations. They included farmers, coal miners, train drivers, policemen, fire fighters and some civil servants.

The government in Britain was afraid that the Germans would invade Britain and take over the country. The men who stayed at home were asked to join the Home Guard to defend Britain in case of a German invasion.

At first, the Home Guard did not have weapons or uniforms. They had to train with picks and crowbars because they had no guns. Many people made fun of the men in the Home Guard because of this. In the early part of the war they would not have been able to protect Britain from a German attack. Later, however, weapons and equipment were sent to the Home Guard from America.

This photograph shows Home Guard volunteers in 1940. They have no weapons or uniforms. They have tried to turn the car into a kind of tank.

As well as the Home Guard, there were other jobs that men in Britain could volunteer for. These included fire fighters (in case of bomb attacks), Special Police (to help the police force), the Royal Observer Corps (to watch for enemy planes), and the Air Raid Precaution (ARP) wardens (to help people during bomb attacks). In some of these jobs, men and women worked side by side. However, not all men were happy about this.

Men and women worked as ARP wardens to help rescue people after air raids.

 This is part of a letter written to the *Bolton Daily Mail* in 1941:

When I enrolled as a Special Constable, I felt that I had at least volunteered for a man's job.

From the *Daily Mail* I am surprised and almost disgusted to see that Bolton has just appointed its first woman Special Constable. Is there nothing sacred to man?

For my part I shall not attend any lectures or instruction classes at which there are women. In fact, I am considering resigning.

Key ideas

air raid
defence

invasion
reserved occupations

The home front

1. What message is given by the poster at the top of page 12?
2. Describe what the man is wearing in the poster.
3. Describe what the men are wearing in the photograph at the bottom of page 12.
4. Write a list of the differences between the poster and the photograph.
5. What do you think has happened in the photograph of the Home Guard?
6. Men and women worked together as ARP wardens. How well do you think this worked? Give reasons for your answer.
7. Write a letter to the *Bolton Daily Mail* in reply to the Special Constable.

The war at home

Find out what it was like to be a member of the Home Guard or the ARP.

1. Do you think the men of the Home Guard and the ARP did an important job? Why?
2. How do you think the men of the Home Guard felt when people made fun of them?
3. What was the main job of ARP wardens? Why was this so important?
4. What happened to the Home Guard in 1944? Why?

This type of air-raid shelter was called an Anderson shelter. It was named after the man who designed it.

The government believed that a German attack would happen at night. It was important that German planes could not see anything on the ground that they could bomb, so the 'blackout' began. All street lights were turned off at night. Every house, shop and office building had thick black curtains to stop light getting out. Cars had special shields over their headlights. A group called the Air Raid Precaution (ARP) wardens made sure that everyone obeyed the blackout. They also helped the ambulance service and the fire brigade during air raids.

Members of the Home Guard, like this man in 1940, were volunteer soldiers who protected Britain against a German invasion.

6.
Defending Britain

During the Second World War, British people became frightened of a German invasion. In June 1940 Germany occupied France, and German troops reached the Channel. Britain was left to face Germany alone. Everyone prepared for an attack. Tank traps and look-out posts were built all around the country, but especially in the south and along the coastline. Church bells had to stay silent – they were to be rung only if the enemy invaded, to warn everyone what was happening.

Everyone in Britain had to prepare for a German attack. The blackout did not stop the German bombers – it just made their job more difficult. To be safe from the bombs, people built air-raid shelters in their gardens. When the air-raid siren sounded, people rushed into their shelters and stayed there until the end of the raid. People without shelters had to hide under the stairs or use public shelters.

The large gas mask was used for babies, the red mask was given to children, and the mask in the front was used by adults. The wooden rattle was used to warn people of poison gas, and the bell was rung when the gas had been cleared away.

The government in Britain believed that the Germans would use poison gas during their bombing raids. Everyone in Britain was given a gas mask. Whenever an air-raid siren sounded, people put on their gas masks to stop themselves being poisoned, even if they were inside an air-raid shelter. There were Mickey Mouse gas masks for children and special masks for babies.

 The government gave lots of warnings about air raids:

If you hear the rattle when you are out, put on your gas mask at once and get indoors as soon as you can. Keep off the streets until the poison gas has been cleared away.

Life on the home front

Life in Britain during the war was not easy, especially during air raids.

1. Find out what it was like in an air-raid shelter.
2. Imagine you lived in Britain during the war. Write about what it was like during an air raid — the sirens, going to the shelter, putting on your gas mask, and so on.

Preparing for raids

1. Why did the government think it was important to have ARP wardens?
2. Why was it important for ARP wardens to be well trained?
3. Why was a blackout important at night?
4. What is the Anderson shelter made from? Why is it partly buried in the garden?
5. Why did people need to use shelters like this?
6. What do you think the man from the Home Guard is looking for? Why?
7. Why were gas masks important in the war?
8. What were the two main things people had to do if there was an air raid?

Key ideas

air raid   invasion
defence

7. Evacuation

All wars are a time of saying goodbye. At the beginning of the Second World War in 1939, the first people to say goodbye were children, not soldiers. The government was afraid that the Germans would bomb British towns and cities. On the morning of Friday 1st September, two days before the war began, thousands of children were sent home from school to pack, ready to be evacuated to the countryside.

Many children were happy in the countryside with their new 'foster parents' and stayed until the war was over. However, some children were very unhappy.

Buildings destroyed in the Blitz in 1942. Children were evacuated to save them from being killed or injured in their homes.

The Germans did not bomb Britain as everyone expected, and by January 1940 three out of every four evacuees had gone home. To stop this, the government used posters to warn people and gave parents cheap train tickets to visit their children. However, it was only when bombing began in September 1940 that children began to be evacuated again.

 Joe, aged nine, was evacuated from London in 1939:

I paraded with all the other children from the station. On one side I had a gas mask in a box, on the other side I had a haversack full of sandwiches and apples. In my pocket were labels showing my school, my address and my destination. In one hand I had a suitcase of clothes, in the other some comics.

Hundreds of children were evacuated from London in 1939.

The Blitz

In September 1940 the Germans began to bomb the main towns and cities in Britain.

1. Why was this bombing called the Blitz?
2. Pretend you are a child who has not been evacuated. Write a letter to a friend who has been evacuated, explaining what it is like still living in a town.
3. Now pretend you are an evacuated child. Write a letter to a friend still living in a town. Describe your new home and how you feel.

This government poster encouraged mothers to send their children to the countryside.

Leaving home

1. Why were children evacuated?
2. Why do you think some children returned home after a few months?
3. Copy and complete this chart. Write at least three points under each heading.

Evacuation	
Good things	Bad things

4. Look at the photograph of the evacuated child on page 16. How do you think he feels? Would you feel like this if you were being evacuated?
5. Look at the picture of the bombed buildings. Write a list of reasons why the government wanted children to move to the countryside.
6. Look at the poster. What do you think the boy in the poster is trying to do? What does the man want him to do instead? Why?

Key ideas

Blitz   evacuation

8. Britain and Europe

This special fifty pence coin was minted in 1973 to celebrate Britain joining the EEC.

When the Second World War ended in 1945 there were still many problems in Europe. Towns and cities all over Europe had been destroyed. Millions of people had been killed. The war had cost a lot of money and many countries were very poor. The Prime Minister of Britain during the war, Winston Churchill, wanted the countries of Europe to join together in a 'United States of Europe'. He hoped this would help the countries to recover from the war and prevent any future wars.

In 1957 six European countries formed the European Economic Community (EEC). The main aim of the EEC was to allow more business between the countries of Europe. It also allowed people to travel more easily between the countries. Since then other countries have joined, and more have asked to join.

In 1973 the British government, led by Prime Minister Edward Heath, decided that Britain should join the EEC. A special fifty pence coin was minted in Britain to celebrate.

 Winston Churchill made a famous speech about Europe in 1946:

We must build a kind of United States of Europe. Time may be short. At present there is a breathing space, but if we are to form a United States of Europe – or whatever name it may take – then we must begin now.

 A new Europe

1. When was the EEC formed?
2. When did Britain join?
3. Who decided that Britain should join?

The EU headquarters in Brussels, Belgium.

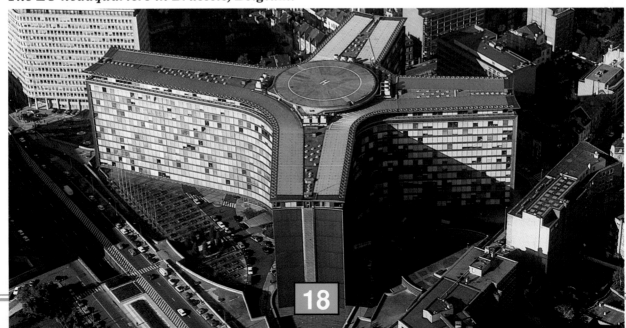

The European Parliament at Strasbourg.

The EEC is now called the EU (European Union). The EU has its own parliament. The European Parliament has members from each country of the EU and passes laws which the member countries have to follow. The Members of the European Parliament (MEPs) are chosen by an election in each country. They meet at the European Parliament headquarters in Strasbourg.

There are now 16 countries in the EU, and more countries are hoping to join. Some people still like Winston Churchill's idea of a 'United States of Europe', with all the countries joined together under one government. However, not everyone wants this because it would take away the power of each country. It also means that each country would have to obey the rules decided by the other countries.

Uniting Europe

The EEC was formed in 1957 for many different reasons. It is growing as more countries join, but not everyone agrees with it.

1. Who were the first six members of the EEC?
2. Do you think it is important for the countries of Europe to be joined together in this way? Why?
3. Why is the EEC now called the EU?
4. How do you think the aims of the EU might have changed since 1957?
5. Why do you think some people disagree with the EU?

Key ideas

election   parliament

9. Immigration

Immigrants arriving in Britain in the 1960s.

In the years after the Second World War there were plenty of jobs in Britain, but not enough people to do them. To fill these jobs, the government asked people in other countries to come to Britain.

Many of the people who came to Britain were from countries once ruled by Britain, such as the West Indies and India. These people had strong links with Britain – for example, many of them held British passports.

People who move to another country to live and work are called immigrants. Immigrants to Britain settled in the large industrial towns of northern England, the West Midlands and in London. They thought they would be welcome in Britain and would have comfortable lives.

	1950s	1960s	1970s	1980s
West Indies	405,000	328,000	29,000	10,000
India	30,000	332,000	80,000	52,000
Pakistan	17,000	144,000	86,000	66,000
Bangladesh	—	—	22,000	50,000
East Africa	—	6,000	118,000	23,000
Others	46,000	125,000	98,000	281,000
TOTAL	498,000	935,000	433,000	482,000

This chart shows the number of people who moved to Britain between 1950 and 1989.

An immigrant searching for somewhere to live in 1958.

by passing laws to make it more difficult for people to move to Britain. They also wanted to ensure that immigrants who had already arrived were treated fairly. The Immigration Act of 1962 limited the number of immigrants who could enter Britain each year. However, this did not solve the problems. Racism continued.

Many people moved to Britain before the Act was passed because they thought it would be difficult to get in afterwards.

1960	57,700
1961	115,150
1962	119,770
1963	63,000
1964	53,140
1965	51,200

This chart shows how the Immigration Act of 1962 affected the number of immigrants to Britain.

New immigrants to Britain were often badly treated. Many of them found it hard to get work and had to take poorly paid jobs. Landlords often refused to rent rooms to them. People who already lived in Britain were often rude or violent to immigrants.

People who make judgements about others based on race, colour of skin or religion are racist. The government tried to ease the problems of racism

Brave new world

Find out more about immigration and racism in Britain.

1. Use an atlas to find which countries immigrants to Britain came from.
2. What happened to the number of immigrants in the 1970s and 1980s? Why?
3. Do you think racism is still a problem in Britain? Give reasons for your answer.

Moving to Britain

1. Why did immigrants come to Britain?
2. Why did they settle in industrial areas?
3. Why were there so many immigrants to Britain in the early 1960s?
4. Look at the photograph at the top of this page. Why has this notice been put in the window?
5. Write a list of words which you think describe the feelings of the people in the photographs on these pages.

Key ideas

immigration
racism

Second World War

10. The Welfare State

During the Second World War, the government asked Sir William Beveridge and a group of experts to examine living standards in Britain, including poverty, education, employment, health and housing.

In August 1945 the Second World War ended. A new government was elected in Britain, led by the Labour Party. The new government, under the new Prime Minister, Clement Attlee, decided to set up a welfare state in Britain to follow the recommendations of the Beveridge Report.

Poverty

The 1948 National Assistance Act gave payments to the poor and needy.

National Insurance

In 1946 the National Insurance Act said that everyone should pay part of their wages to the welfare state.

Health

The 1946 National Health Service Act gave free medical treatment to all.

The Welfare State

In 1942 the Beveridge Report said a welfare state was needed 'from the cradle to the grave'.

Sir William Beveridge

Education

The 1944 Education Act gave free education to all. From 1947, the school leaving age was 15.

Families

The 1945 Family Allowance Act gave money to parents to help them bring up their children.

Unemployment

From 1946, every adult in Britain without a job was given money by the government, called unemployment benefit.

This chart shows the main parts of the Welfare State and the main effect of each part.

One of the most important parts of the Welfare State was the National Health Service (NHS), which gave free medical treatment to everyone. The NHS was very successful in many areas. For example, it helped to reduce the number of children who died from illnesses that could be easily prevented.

During the election in 1950, the Labour Party used posters about the Welfare State to persuade people to vote for them.

A Labour Party election poster, 1950.

This chart shows the number of children who died in York between 1930 and 1960.

 A new way of life

Find out more about how the Welfare State changed the British way of life in the 1940s.

1. What was the school leaving age before 1947?
2. Write a list of questions to ask an adult aged over 50 about the difference the Welfare State made to their lives.

 Quality of life

1. How did the Family Allowance Act help people?
2. Why was the NHS so important?
3. What might have happened to a poor sick person before 1946?
4. Why do you think the number of child deaths in York went down between 1930 and 1960?
5. Look at the poster on this page. Who produced the poster? Who is it aimed at?

 Key ideas

election	poverty
living standards	Welfare State

11. Houses and Homes

Semi-detached houses built in the 1930s.

In the 1930s some houses in Britain had not changed for over a hundred years. Many families shared a house with no indoor toilet or bathroom. Houses were close together with no gardens and very little light or fresh air.

Some new houses were built in the 1930s, but they were expensive and many ordinary people could not afford them.

In the 1950s many local councils began to clear away bad houses. They began to build estates of houses with gardens. For the first time, ordinary families could buy their own home. New houses were built with electricity, indoor bathrooms and toilets.

However, building new estates did not solve all the problems of bad housing. There were many people living in large towns and cities, but there was not enough land to build houses.

An advertisement for new homes in the 1930s.

 New homes

1. Look at the photographs of 1930s houses. Do you think these new houses were popular with everyone?
2. Why did councils need to build new houses?
3. Do you think it was a good idea to build houses with gardens and more space? Why?
4. Why is it important for everyone to have things like electricity, water and a bathroom?
5. What do you think it is like to live at the top of a block of flats? Do you think it would be a good or a bad place to live?

A large block of flats in London.

Key ideas

detached   semi-detached

In the 1950s and 1960s many councils decided to build blocks of flats instead of houses. These could be built quickly and cheaply. They took up a small amount of land and gave homes to lots of people.

Many people thought flats like this were the answer to housing problems. People were happy to live somewhere clean and healthy, but soon they had to face new problems. Children who lived in flats high off the ground had nowhere to play. People who lived alone could feel very lonely.

Today, many people still live in high-rise blocks of flats. However, many blocks have been knocked down. Most new homes built today are semi-detached and detached houses on small local developments.

Many blocks of flats have been demolished to make way for traditional houses.

 A change for the better?

Houses and homes have been built in many shapes and sizes in Britain since 1930.

1. Do you think it was a good idea to build blocks of flats to house lots of people? Why?
2. Why have many of these flats been demolished?
3. In the 1950s and 1960s 'new towns' were built to move people out of crowded cities. Write a list of these new towns.

12. Religious Change

In the 1930s and 1940s Christianity was an important part of life in Britain. Many families attended a church every Sunday. The local church was a very important part of life in towns and villages.

Going to church

1. Look at the photograph of the congregation in church. What does this tell you about what it was like going to church in the 1930s?
2. Would you have liked going to a church like this? Give two reasons.
3. Do you think William Jones enjoyed going to church?
4. What has happened to some churches since William's time?
5. What has happened to the church in the photograph below? Why?
6. Why do you think fewer people go to church today? Give two reasons.

A congregation in a church in 1934.

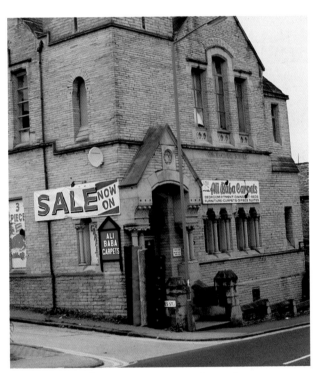

Many churches are now used as shops.

 This is how William Jones from Cardiff described going to church in 1934:

A stiff white shirt, a tie, a suit with shiny shoes and hair greased flat. A sixpence for the collection plate. Don't be late. Inside the air was cold and musty. Don't look round, eyes front. At 10 o'clock there was silence. The church was full, each family in its place, the same place every Sunday.

In recent years going to church has become less popular. Many people think religion is not a very important part of their lives. Only one in every ten people now go to a Christian church every Sunday. Many churches have been sold and are now used as shops, offices or even homes.

Britain is a multi-cultural country. People from many different religions can be found in Britain. Christians and Jews have been in Britain for a very long time, but others such as Muslims, Sikhs and Hindus have come to Britain since the 1930s.

Key ideas

festival   tradition

Religious belief can affect every aspect of life, including the way people dress.

Some of the religions which have become popular in Britain since 1930 include Sikhism, Hinduism, Islam and Buddhism. As these different religious groups became popular, they introduced new traditions and festivals. For example, Diwali is a Hindu festival of lights which celebrates the story of Prince Rama and his beautiful wife, Sita. The use of lights at Diwali is similar to the use of lights at the Christian festival of Christmas. For many religions in Britain, light is a symbol of happiness, goodness and rejoicing.

New religions

Find out more about the religions that have become popular in Britain since 1930.

1. Draw a time line to show which religions first became popular in Britain.
2. Find out about some more religious festivals. Choose one festival and write about it in detail.
3. Draw and complete a chart to show:
   - the main religions in Britain today
   - the main festivals of each religion
   - the holy book of each religion
   - the main symbol of each religion.

Ladies' fashions, 1937

People have always followed fashion in the clothes they wear and the way they wear them. In the 1930s, clothes were different from those worn today. Women wore long dresses and men wore suits. Many people wore hats.

War fashions, 1943.

During the Second World War clothes were difficult to buy. Fashion became less important. People mended their clothes to make them last.

13. Clothes Line

Popular fashions, 1994.

In the 1990s casual clothes are still fashionable, often with certain 'labels' which help to sell the clothes.

Key idea

fashion

Rock 'n' roll, 1955

In the 1950s fashion began to change. The 'Teddy Boy' style was popular, which had knee-length jackets and drainpipe trousers. Women wore long skirts with bright colours and patterns.

Mini skirts, 1969

In the 1960s 'mini-skirts' were very popular. Denim jeans, shirts and jackets became fashionable.

Casual wear, 1982.

In the 1980s fashion became more casual, with sweatshirts, tracksuits and leggings becoming popular.

Flares, 1976

In the 1970s bright colours and flared trousers were very popular.

Changing fashions

1. Choose one of the fashions from these pages. What does it tell you about life in Britain at the time?
2. What do changes in fashion tell you about the change in British life since 1930?
3. Which fashions have come and gone quickly and which have lasted? Why do you think this is so?
4. Find out more about some of the fashions mentioned on this page, such as Teddy boys or flares.
5. Collect some photographs of the fashions on these pages to make a fashion time line.

14. Pop Music

Cliff Richard in 1958.

Bill Hayley and the Comets.

In the 1950s people began to listen to new kinds of music. Young people began to listen to rock 'n' roll, instead of the slow dance music that their parents had enjoyed.

Young people liked rock 'n' roll because it was loud and fast. New dances such as the jive became popular with rock 'n' roll. In 1955 Bill Hayley and the Comets recorded their song 'Rock Around the Clock'. This became the most famous rock 'n' roll song of all time. Other famous singers included Elvis Presley, Chuck Berry and Cliff Richard.

For the first time in the 1950s, records were made cheaper and people could afford to buy them. Cheap record players were also made for the first time. These changes meant that 'pop music' became more popular throughout the 1950s.

The Beatles.

In the 1960s the Beatles became a very popular group. People called them the 'Fab Four' because they were so famous. They were John Lennon, Paul McCartney, George Harrison and Ringo Starr. During the 1960s they made over thirty hit records. Other pop groups in the 1960s included the Kinks, the Animals and the Rolling Stones.

Throughout the 1960s television played an important part in making pop music popular, with programmes like *Ready Steady Go* and *Juke Box Jury*. Cliff Richard continued to make records in the 1960s and became a superstar.

Key ideas

pop music   superstar

The Osmonds.

Wham!

Cliff Richard in 1989.

In the 1970s rock music was still popular, but people also began to listen to other kinds of music. Styles like punk and reggae became popular.

Pop groups like the Osmonds and the Bay City Rollers attracted groups of teenage fans called 'teenyboppers'. Despite the changing styles of music, Cliff Richard continued to sell millions of records.

In the 1980s electronic music and computerised keyboards became popular. Superstars such as Duran Duran, Madonna and Wham! sold millions of records.

In the late 1980s, records and tapes were gradually replaced by compact discs, which were much smaller and gave a much clearer sound. Through all these changes, Cliff Richard continued to be popular.

Loud and proud

Pop music has changed in many different ways since the 1950s.

1. Collect some photographs of pop groups from 1950 to 1980. Make a display showing how pop music has changed.
2. Listen to a pop record from the 1950s, and then one from the 1980s. How are they different? Are they the same in any way?
3. Why do you think Cliff Richard has stayed popular since the 1950s?

Rock around the clock

1. Look at the photographs of pop stars. Write a list of the ways in which pop music changed in each decade.
2. List some of the pop groups that became famous in the 1950s.
3. Why did these groups become popular?
4. How did the style of pop music change during the 1960s?
5. What was different about pop stars in the 1970s?
6. What happened to records and tapes in the 1980s? Why?

15. Radio and Television

In 1930 radio was popular in Britain. Radio programmes could be heard in most parts of the country. By 1939 eight out of every ten families in Britain owned a radio.

A radio from the 1930s.

When the Second World War began in 1939, people listened to their radios for news of what was happening. The radio was an important way to keep people cheerful during the war.

In 1936 the first television sets were put on sale. They had very small screens – about 25cm across – and they were set in big wooden cabinets. The first programmes could be seen only by people who lived within 90km of the transmitter in north London. At 3 o'clock on 2nd November 1936, the BBC began the first regular television service in the world.

One of the first television sets.

This was what people saw on the first day of BBC television:
- 3.00pm – opening speech by the Postmaster General (the man in charge of television)
- 3.15pm – interval
- 3.20pm – news and comedy
- 4.00pm – close

 TV times

Find out about how television programmes have changed since the 1940s.

1. Make a list of favourite television programmes from the 1940s and 1950s.
2. Make a list of favourite television programmes of today.
3. How have programmes changed in this time?

By 1937 2,000 sets were in use. Almost 5,000 sets had been sold by the end of 1938 and 20,000 by 1939. When the Second World War began in September 1939 BBC television closed down.

The BBC opened two more radio stations in the 1940s. In 1967 Radio 1 was opened, as well as 22 local BBC radio stations. Commercial radio stations began broadcasting in the 1970s. There are now over 100 of them.

1936	Televisions went on sale. The BBC broadcast the first programmes.
1939	BBC television closed down.
1945	BBC television began broadcasting again.
1955	Commercial television began broadcasting.
1964	BBC2 began broadcasting.
1967	Colour television used for the first time.
1974	First CEEFAX transmission.
1982	Channel 4 began broadcasting.
1987	Satellite television began broadcasting.

The main changes in television since 1936.

Look and listen

1. Look at the photograph of the radio. How is different from the ones used today?
2. Describe the television in the photograph. Do you think it would have been easy to watch? Give reasons for your answer.
3. Why was radio important to people in Britain during the war?
4. When was the first television broadcast? How long did it last?
5. Look at the list of changes in television since 1936. Decide which of these changes was the most important, and then write out the list again, putting the most important at the top and the least important at the bottom.

In the late 1940s and 1950s television became more popular. By 1949 344,000 people owned a television set. In 1952 a transmitter was opened in Scotland, and most of the country could receive television.

Even though more and more people began to watch television in the 1940s and 1950s, radio was still popular.

Key ideas

broadcast   commercial

Inside a modern television studio.

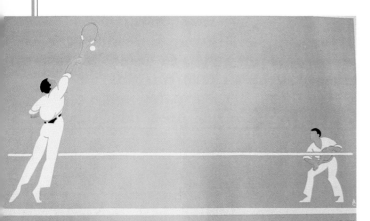

An advertisement for Wimbledon, 1936.

FOR THE WIMBLEDON TOURNAMENT JUNE 25th
NEAREST STATION SOUTHFIELDS
SPECIAL BUSES TO & FROM THE STATION AND GROUND

16. Sport

Roger Bannister ran a mile in less than four minutes in 1954.

Sport has always played a very important part in British life. In the 1930s tennis was very popular in Britain. British players were very successful at Wimbledon. Fred Perry won the men's singles title three times, and Dorothy Round won the women's singles twice. Since then the competition has been won mostly by players from America and Europe.

In July 1948 the Olympic Games were held in Britain. It involved nearly 5,000 competitors from 59 countries. Britain was still repairing the damage from the Second World War, so most of the competitors had to stay in army barracks and colleges, unlike the specially built Olympic villages of today.

For many years athletes had tried to run a mile in less than four minutes. On 6th May 1954 Roger Bannister broke the four-minute barrier. His time of 3 minutes 59.4 seconds gave him a place in sporting history.

 Sport in Britain

1. How many times did British players win at Wimbledon in the 1930s?
2. Why was Roger Bannister important?
3. Look at the photograph of Ian Botham on page 35. Why was this cricket match important?
4. Look at the information on England winning the World Cup. How are the the memories of the two football fans different?
5. What is the footballer in the photograph holding in his hand? Why?

Cricket is another important British sport. Famous cricket players include Fred Truman, Geoffrey Boycott and Denis Compton. One of the most famous cricket matches of recent years was the 'Ashes' match between England and Australia in 1981. England won the match, even though everyone expected them to lose.

Football is a very popular sport all over Britain. It is the most popular sport on television. One of the most important football events in Britain was England's World Cup victory in July 1966.

 England won the World Cup in 1966. This is how one man remembers it:

I remember seeing it on the television in black and white. It was a brilliant game, England were 2-0 up at half time but it ended up going into extra time. The third England goal bounced off the crossbar and straight into the net. England's fourth came right at the end.

 Another football fan remembers the same match in a different way:

I'll never forget, it was 3rd August 1966 when we won the World Cup, in front of a crowd of 100,000. The teams were drawing one-all at half time and two-all at full time. In extra time Hurst scored his hat-trick. Our fourth goal finished them off.

Ian Botham helped England to win the Ashes in 1981.

Fun and games

Find out more about sport in Britain since 1930.

1. Collect some information on great moments in sport since 1930. Make a collage for display showing how things have changed.
2. Write a short newspaper story with a headline. Choose one of the sports from these pages, or choose another sport you are interested in.

England won the World Cup in 1966.

17. Holidays

In the 1930s some people went on holiday to boarding houses or guest houses at the seaside. Holidaymakers had their own bedroom but usually shared a bathroom with other guests. Landlords and landladies often asked their guests to leave the boarding house every morning and would not let them return until the end of the day, even if it was raining.

An advertisement for the Butlin's camp at Clacton-on-Sea.

Billy Butlin did not like holidays like this. He decided that people should have a different kind of holiday, so he invented the holiday camp. One of his first holiday camps was opened at Skegness in 1936. It had rows of cabins for 1,000 campers. The activities included swimming and playing tennis. Many people travelled to the holiday camps by train.

Friday, August 22nd, 1947

7.30am	Holy Communion
9.30am	Kiddies' Playtime
10.00am	Keep Fit
10.00am	Parents' Free Hour
10.00am	Bowls
10.30am	Fishing at the Lake
11.00am	All-Day Cricket Match
11.00am	Tombola
11.00am	Dress Rehearsal for the Campers' Concert
11.00am	Swimming and Diving Lessons
11.00am	Dancing Class for Adults
2.00pm	Bowls
2.15pm	Parents' Free Hour
2.30pm	Junior Campers Concert
2.45pm	'They Walk Alone' – play at the Butlin Theatre
4.00pm	Tea Dance
5.30pm	Presentation of Prizes
7.45pm	Whist Drive
7.45pm	Campers' Concert
8.30pm	Dancing
10.00pm	Penny-On-The-Drum
11.45pm	'Au Revoir' by the Redcoats
Midnight	Goodnight Campers

A list of activities at a Butlin's camp in 1947.

Getting away from it all

1. Do you think that boarding houses were nice places to stay?
2. In what way were holiday camps different?
3. Would people have enjoyed the activities at Butlins in 1947? Why?
4. Do you think the advertisement for the Butlin's camp is attractive? Would it work today?
5. In what way is the modern holiday brochure different from the 1961 brochure?
6. Travelling by aeroplane is a popular way of going on holiday. Write a list of places people can go by aeroplane in just a few hours.

Airports like this one at Gatwick have made holidays abroad much easier and cheaper.

In the 1960s people began to spend more money on holidays. Many people no longer wanted holidays in Britain, mainly because of the weather. Package holidays became popular – people arranged holidays through a travel agent, and they paid one price which included the cost of travelling, the hotel and meals. In the 1970s and 1980s air travel became cheaper, and now it is easy to take a holiday in almost any part of the world.

A holiday brochure from 1961.

A holiday brochure from 1994.

Different kinds of holiday

Find out more about different kinds of holiday.

1. Write a list of the main differences between a boarding house holiday, a holiday camp and a foreign hotel.
2. Collect postcards from people on holiday and put them on a map. Find out how they travelled and where they stayed.

Key idea

package holiday

18. Transport

In the 1930s most ordinary people travelled by train. Most towns were linked by railways, and trains were a cheap and easy way of travelling. However, in 1963 the government decided that the railways were losing too much money. Many stations were closed and many train services were stopped. People had to find other means of transport. For example, in 1938 there were almost 7,000 railway stations in Britain, but in 1992 there were less than 2,400.

A traffic jam.

A modern Intercity train.

In the 1950s and 1960s fewer people travelled by train. Instead, people began to travel by car. Many new roads were built. Bypasses were built to take traffic away from busy town centres. Motorways were built to join large towns and cities. Britain's first motorway was the M1 between London and Birmingham, which was opened in 1959.

There are now almost 30,000 kilometres of motorway in Britain, and more are being built all the time. There are often traffic jams on motorways, especially because of roadworks or accidents.

However, trains still travelled between large towns and cities in Britain. In 1966 the first Intercity train was used, which could travel much more quickly than old steam or diesel trains. Many trains now run using electricity, which is much quieter and cleaner.

Key idea

passenger aeroplane

During the 1930s, very few people travelled by aeroplane. Most people who wanted to travel to other countries went by ship. This took a long time and was very expensive, and so few people could afford to travel in this way.

The first jet aeroplane to carry passengers was called the Comet. It began a regular passenger service in 1952. This was a small jet that could not carry many people. Since then passenger aeroplanes have become much larger. Modern jumbo jets can carry more than 500 people.

The fastest passenger aeroplane in the world is Concorde. It was built by Britain and France and began flying in 1976. It can fly at about 2,100 kilometres per hour. Although modern aeroplanes like this are very fast, they are also very noisy, especially for people who live near large airports.

Road, rail and air

1. Why did many people travel by train in the 1930s? Give two reasons.
2. Why do many people travel by car today? Give two reasons.
3. Why have more people started travelling by aeroplane since the 1950s?
4. What can cause a traffic jam on a motorway?
5. Describe how it feels to be stuck in a traffic jam like the one shown in the photograph.
6. Imagine you live in one of the houses underneath the aeroplane in the photograph. Describe how the noise affects your life.

Miles ahead

Think about how transport has changed in Britain since 1930.

1. Draw a chart to show the good and bad things about travelling by train, car and aeroplane.
2. Draw a time line to show how transport has changed in Britain since 1930.

A jumbo jet flying over some houses near an airport.

19. Car Travel

The number of cars in Britain grew quickly in the 1930s. In 1930 there were one million cars on the roads in Britain. By 1939 this had increased to two million. This meant that there were more jobs for people in factories, garages, and building roads.

Factories that made cars in the 1930s were very different from modern factories. Most of the work was done by hand. There were few machines to do all the hard work, and so only a small number of cars could be made.

A car assembly line in the 1990s.

Modern car factories use computers and robots to produce cars quickly and cheaply. This means that many factories can employ fewer staff.

A car assembly line in the 1930s.

Key ideas

assembly line   factory

Date	Workers	Cars
1935	8,000	22,000
1992	10,300	1,594,000

This chart shows the number of people who worked at Vauxhall cars and the number of cars they made.

More and more people began to buy cars in the 1950s. One of the most famous cars of the time was the Morris Minor and later the Mini. The Mini was made by Austin and Morris and cost only £500.

A Morris Minor in 1949.

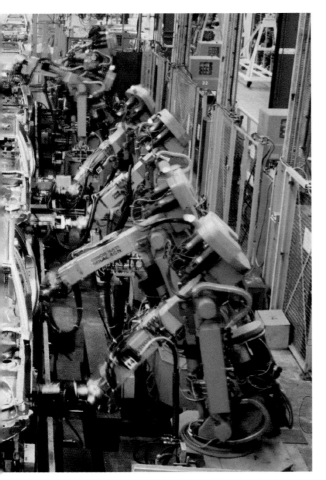

Car manufacturers today bring out new models of car every few years, each one better than the last.

When people choose a new car they consider what it looks like, how fast it can go, and also how much petrol it uses and how expensive it is to run.

Many people are also worried about how cars affect our environment, and so many cars now use unleaded petrol. This helps to stop poisonous gas escaping into the air.

A Mini in 1959.

Car crazy

1. What are the differences between car production in the 1930s and today?
2. What does the chart tell you about the number of cars made between 1935 and 1992?
3. Look carefully at the pictures of the Morris Minor and the Mini. How are these cars different from cars today? Are they similar?

Life in the fast lane

Find out more about cars in Britain since 1930.

1. Collect some photographs and advertisements of cars in the 1930s, and for cars in the 1990s. Make two displays to show how cars have changed.
2. Conduct a survey about cars. Ask five people about their cars — why they bought the car, what they like about it, and so on. Make a database of your findings.

20. Energy

Between 1930 and 1960, most of Britain's energy came from coal. It was used to heat homes, offices and schools. Coal was also used in power stations to make electricity, and as fuel for steam trains.

Key ideas

energy source   unemployment

A coal mine in Wales in the 1950s. South Wales was one of the largest coal mining areas in Britain. The area suffered much hardship and unemployment when many of the mines were closed in the 1960s, 1970s and 1980s.

In the 1940s and 1950s there were hundreds of coal mines in Britain. Gradually, machines were introduced to do many of the jobs that had once been done by hand. This meant that during the 1960s and 1970s many miners were put out of work. The situation became worse in the 1970s when new sources of energy were found, such as oil and gas. In 1955 there were almost 900 coal mines in Britain. In 1994 there were fewer than 20 mines left.

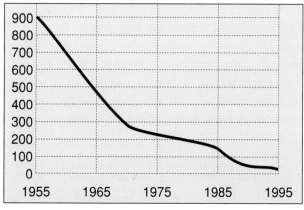

This graph shows how the number of coal mines fell between 1955 and 1995.

In the last 40 years there have been many changes in the way that Britain produces its energy. The first British nuclear power station was opened in the 1950s. In the 1960s and 1970s, alternative energy sources were discovered, including large reserves of oil and gas beneath the North Sea.

A wind farm is a very clean way of producing energy.

An oil rig in the North Sea, which is used to drill for oil and then pump it to the shore.

Nuclear power stations have become unpopular because of the pollution they can cause. Many power stations that use coal, oil and gas also release large amounts of dirt and smoke into the environment.

Many people believe it is now very important to develop cleaner and more efficient ways of producing energy. One way of doing this is on a wind farm, which uses windmills to generate electricity. A wind farm in West Yorkshire has 23 windmills and could provide power for 4,500 homes.

Power points

1. Describe the changes in the way Britain has produced its energy since 1930.
2. Why was the coal industry so important to Britain?
3. Give two reasons why many of Britain's coal mines closed between 1955 and the present day.
4. Write a list of the alternative ways of producing energy that are used in Britain today.

Producing energy

Find out more about how energy has been produced in Britain.

1. What do the terms 'renewable' and 'non-renewable' mean?
2. Write a list of renewable and non-renewable energy sources. What are the advantages and disadvantages of each?

Smog in London, 1952.

The **Braer** *oil disaster, 1993.*

Pollution can also happen at sea. In January 1993 an oil tanker called the *Braer* ran aground off the Shetland Islands. Oil leaked out of the tanker, and after six days an oil slick covered a large area of the sea. A large part of the coastline of Shetland was spoiled when oil was washed up.

21.
Pollution

Pollution has been a problem in Britain for many years. In 1952 thick smog (a mixture of smoke and fog) covered London for four days. The yellow smog was so thick that flares had to be carried in front of buses so that the drivers could see where they were going. The smog even got inside buildings – for example, cinemas had to close because people could not see the screen. The smog also made diseases like bronchitis much worse. Many people died.

 Dirty business

1. What is smog? Why did it kill some people in London in 1952?
2. Look at the photograph of the London smog. Describe what you think it would have been like to live in London at the time.
3. Describe what happened to the *Braer* oil tanker in 1993.
4. Look carefully at the photograph of the *Braer* disaster. What do you think made the oil spread so far?
5. What has happened in the photograph of the forest?
6. Look at the list of facts. Write a list of ways in which these problems could be solved.
7. Design a poster like the anti-litter poster. Use the facts to help you.

In recent years people have become worried about other types of pollution. Look at the facts.

Fact

Radiation from a fire at the Windscale nuclear reactor in 1957 polluted areas of farmland.
In April 1986 the Russian nuclear power station at Chernobyl exploded, sending a poisonous cloud over Britain and other countries. This caused pollution of farmland in Wales, northern England and Scotland.

Fact

In 1986 Britain released 3,760,000 tonnes of sulphur dioxide into the air from power stations. When mixed with moisture in the air it falls as acid rain. This damages lakes, forests and buildings.

Fact

The build-up of gases in the atmosphere is helping to warm up the surface of the Earth. This is called the 'Greenhouse Effect'.

Fact

Gases called CFCs, which are pumped into the air from aerosols and refrigerators, are causing a hole in the ozone layer that protects us all from the Sun's harmful rays. This can lead to serious diseases such as skin cancer.

An anti-litter poster.

Damage caused to a forest by acid rain.

Cleaning up

Find out more about pollution in Britain.

1. What did the government do to make sure that the London smog did not happen again?
2. Carry out an experiment with some oil and sand. Pour a small amount of oil into a tray of sand, and leave it for a few minutes. Describe carefully what has happened to the sand. What effect do you think 50,000 tonnes of oil would have on beaches and wildlife?

Key ideas

atmosphere   radiation
pollution

22.
New Technology

Computers are part of everyday life in Britain. They are used for many things – to help us see distant stars, to stock supermarket shelves, to help fight disease, and to help us tell whether it will be sunny tomorrow. Computers can deal with information much faster than humans.

Charles Babbage invented the computer over a hundred years ago. The first computers worked using cards with holes in them. The first modern electric computer was built in the 1930s. It worked using 'electric valves'. These were faster than the older mechanical computers, but they used a lot of electricity. They were also very expensive to make. They became very hot and often broke down, and they were usually very large – often as big as a whole room!

In the 1950s new kinds of computers were built. They used small transistors instead of electric valves. This meant that computers were cheaper to make, could work faster, used less electricity and took up much less space.

A computer in 1964.

In the 1960s and 1970s computers became cheaper and faster. The silicon chip was invented, which could hold thousands of transistors in a very small space. Silicon chips are very small and very thin, and meant that a new kind of computer could be made: the micro-computer.

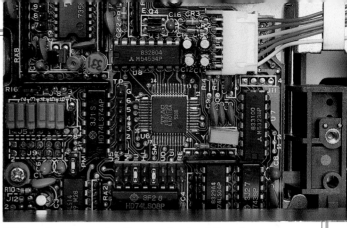

This photograph shows the inside of a modern computer.

Computers are used in many ways at home.

Micro-computers were made smaller and cheaper in the 1970s and 1980s. Many computers are now used in homes and offices. Silicon chips can be found in hundreds of things, such as toys, televisions and washing machines. Almost every part of life in Britain since 1930 has been changed by computers.

 Everyday life with computers

Think about how we use computers every day.

1. Carry out a survey at home or in school. Write a list of everyday things which use silicon chips. Use your information to make a computer database.
2. What do you think computers will be used for in the future?

Key idea

new technology

 Changing computers

1. Who invented the first computer? How did it work?
2. Explain how the invention of each of these things changed computers: the electric valve, the transistor, the silicon chip.
3. What happened to computers in the 1970s and 1980s? Why?
4. How is the computer in the photograph from the 1960s different from the one in your classroom?
5. What is the home computer in the photograph used for?
6. What are computers being used for in the photograph of the office?

Computers are used in many ways in offices.

Glossary

air raid
a bombing attack by enemy aeroplanes

assembly line
a way of making many things one after another, eg cars

atmosphere
a protective layer of gases around the Earth

Blitz
German bombing of Britain in the Second World War

broadcast
sending a radio or television programme

commercial
a radio or television service showing advertisements

defence
to protect or look after something

depression
when a country is poor and people are out of work

detached
a house which is not joined to another house

election
when people choose someone to represent them

energy source
something which can be used to produce energy, eg coal, oil, gas

equal pay
men and women given the same wage for the same job

evacuation
moving to another place in an emergency, eg war

factory
a place which makes things, eg cars

fashion
a certain style of clothes or way of behaving

festival
a celebration, eg a religious event such as Christmas

immigration
moving from one country to another country

invasion
one country taking over another country

living standards
how people measure their quality of life

munitions
military equipment, eg bullets and guns

new technology
developing new ways of doing things, eg with computers

package holiday
a holiday which includes everything in one price

parliament
an assembly of the representatives of a country

passenger aeroplane
an aeroplane that can carry many people

Phoney War
the beginning of the Second World War in 1939 when people in Britain thought the war was not real

pollution
damage to the world around us, eg with smoke

pop music
popular music, sold as records, tapes or compact discs

poverty
lack of money, eg for proper food or clothes

propaganda
trying to make people believe something by giving them lots of information

racism
treating someone badly because of the country they were born in, their skin colour, or their religion

radiation
a poisonous substance found in nuclear power stations which can cause pollution if it escapes

rationing
to share items such as food in a time of crisis, eg war

reserved occupations
certain jobs during the Second World War that men could do instead of joining the army, eg firemen

Second World War
a war which lasted from September 1939 to August 1945 and involved every continent

semi-detached
a house that is joined to another house on one side

spy
a person who keeps a secret watch on other people

superstar
someone who is very famous

tradition
an event or celebration passed down over many years

unemployment
lack of work

welfare state
a system in which the government provides free health care, education, and so on